The WIND Also Sings

The WIND Also Sings

*Poetry of protest
and anger from India's Northeast*

YUMLAM TANA

PARTRIDGE
A Penguin Random House Company

To order additional copies of this book, contact
Partridge India
000 800 10062 62
orders.india@partridgepublishing.com

www.partridgepublishing.com/india

CONTENTS

1. No Clever English.................................1
2. A Tribal Man Speaks 2
3. On Leaving the Village........................5
4. My Brother, You Live in the City 8
5. Tomorrow.....................................10
6. A Dirge from the North-East..................12
7. Who Are We?..................................17
8. A Trophy Poem 22
9. Iguana 24
10. I Will Tell You Why We Are Angry.............26
11. To Our Benevolent Masters 28
12. When an Indian from the Mainland Is Knifed
    in Australia.................................31
13. Will I Hear the Jew's Harp Again? 34
14. 1962 37
15. I Knew of a Place in the Mountains 39
16. More Vignettes 45
17. The Upstart..................................49
18. Journey to Tibet.............................52
19. Yai..60
20. The Role Model...............................62
21. Song of the Driftwoods 64
22. Peter Pan....................................66
23. A Requiem for the Dead.......................68

24. Maybe This Man 71
25. Mollycoddled Little Children 72
26. At Night I See the Beast Stalking the Hills 73
27. The Vandals Broke in and Ransacked My Place 74
28. Like the Sap of a Tuber Plant....................................75
29. The Feather of the Hornbill......................................76
30. Dawki...77
31. Myth Making 78
32. Dead Fish 80
33. Euthanasia...82
34. A Village Belle's Love Letter 83
35. Between You and Me...86
36. An Irreligious Man Conscious of His Sins 91
37. Cul-de-Sac 92
38. The Old Fart..94
39. Let's Hope Anyway...97
40. To Bo Senior 98

For Yajum Lombi

And for Bo Senior, who I believe did not live in vain.

PREFACE

In circa 1947, when the English left the country for good, the native Indian government took over from them and incorporated many of the tribes living in the fringe areas of their territory into their folds—thus also ensuring that others do not get them. Its leadership sold to the credulous tribes the idea that there would be space for all in the sun under the banner of a new nationhood. The catchphrase was 'Unity in diversity'. It worked very well. The tribes readily resigned themselves to this new concept of living under a government with complicated rules and regulations. And soon enough, they began to see themselves as Indians as any other citizen of the country. They also started to have huge expectations from the central government that ruled the country from New Delhi with firm hands. They believed that finally peace, progress, and social justice would reach their doorstep.

The pace of political and administrative growth quickened, which culminated in 20 February 1987 when Arunachal Pradesh was formally inaugurated as the twenty-fourth state of the Indian Union.

But before that in 1962, the two Asian giants, China and India, fought a brief but very bitter war with each other over the question of the territorial status of Arunachal Pradesh. The People's Republic of China claim that the state is a disputed territory and is mostly referred by them as being part of south Tibet. It has soured the relation between the two most powerful actors in the geopolitical scenario of the subcontinent.

In the last few decades, the state of Arunachal Pradesh has seen so many changes, both positive and negative. For instance, globalization and Internet technology has had such a deep impact on the people of the state, whose second or third generations only have been to schools and learnt to read and write. Electoral politics has permeated to the villages, nay seeped into the very psyche of the villagers, where it has become a convention, a necessity to be associated with a political party and thereby, to seek largesse and other benefits that come from it. Village life has disintegrated with the coming up of modern towns and cities as people flock to them in search of better urban amenities and higher standard of living. Learning the English language and the Hindi has acquired dimensions of power and prestige apart from the knowledge that it will open up doors of opportunities in life.

In my poetry, I have tried to examine the questions that are relevant to such a social milieu I belong to as member of my tribe, Nyishi. In this context, poetry to me is about trying to understand my tribal roots and examine the drastic changes that occurred in our short period of history by the extension of civilization, especially the after-effects of postcolonial events from circa 1947.

I studied literature in college and got introduced to all the English poets from Chaucer to Yeats and American poets like Sylvia Plath, Frost, and many others. But the way they were taught in the classrooms killed most of the charm and enjoyment that is usually associated with poetry. It became a stale, academic subject that one had to mug up to sit for the annual examinations. But I fell in love with poetry all over again after reading Darwish, Wislawa Szymborska, and Maya Angelou. In their works, I discovered the missing link that connected the feral and the intellect, the uninhibited expression of the colloquial idioms of the human heart that for me defined what real poetry ought to be, which is to express spontaneously the powerful emotions that we carry in our breast and inspire others through it. After all, poetry is not only an intellectual exercise alone but a love affair of the heart too . . . this labour of love makes me acutely sensitive to the binary opposites of spatial and emotional existence of life; it makes me acutely sensitive to so much of oppressions, injustices, and inequalities all around us even though we delude ourselves to be living in an era that is supposed to be the apogee of human emancipation and liberal democracy. In my own circumstance, I live with the harsh reality of dissent and doubt that threaten to splinter society into exclusive groups of myopic, inward-looking individuals who cannot see the beautiful world beyond their immediate caste and community affiliations. Clearly we have emotional issues, apart from the varied political and social issues, with one another that add so much strain to the tough act of balancing the little options that life has to offer in our quest for the perfect happiness.

The racial discrimination of the people from the north-east by the so-called mainland Indians because of their facial features and food habits and on various other grounds also bothers me. The tag Indian, which sits very comfortably on our psyche, is rudely shaken whenever one of our fellow tribesmen from north-east India are subjected to violence and verbal abuse in the towns and cities of the mainland where they go for pursuing higher education and for medical treatment mostly. A few also try their luck at making a living in the cities of dreams located in mainland India, such as Delhi, Kolkata, Mumbai, and Bangalore, but end up feeling disillusioned with bitterness creeping inside them after being treated like a second-class citizen in their own country. I have tried to address this perennial problem in many of my poems.

'The Wind Also Sings' is also how I perceive myself changing as an individual from the raw teenager who published his first volume of verse *The Man and the Tiger* (Writer's Forum, Ranchi) way back in 1999. These fifteen years I have silently indulged in my secret love affair with poetry only as when my busy schedule as a government official permitted me to do so—I did not want friends and acquaintances smirking at me for being a pseudo-intellectual who dabbles in this 'poetry thing' (as one very senior professor of English literature, who teaches in the local university of my home town and who by the way also happens to be from mainland India, chose to label my leisure pursuit after it was made known to him inadvertently). And as of now, I look forward to writing more poetry in the years to come.

Yumlam Tana

No Clever English

No clever English.
No witty turn of phrases.
I do not have the mind or inclination for any
philosophical discourses.
I do not write to impress people with scholarly
English—
Coining new words isn't my forte.
I am a singer
Who prefers to sing,
Uninhibited
By the laws and lexicons of any language,
Songs full-blooded and feral—
Songs for my people,
Distraught and heartbroken,
Victims of circumstances beyond their ken
And the rapacity of clever people
With education and knowledge.

A Tribal Man Speaks

They say we have always been like this
From the beginning of time,
Unchanging and unyielding—
Very stubborn.
Our language, which has birthed others,
Never reached the sophistry or art
Of the civilized tongue.
Our syntax and grammar are limited
To the speech of the human heart,
Basic and simple,
Just useful enough to sing a lullaby,
Just enough to say I love you;
It seems
Our language never evolved
Beyond its genetic bequest
Of the song, lullaby, and love
And which is why when a tribal woman sings
She can make you laugh and cry
At the same time
And wash you with the nostalgia
Of a white Christmas.
For us, change is something alien.
Why should we change? We are not turncoats.
But nowadays they say tribals can change.

Their votes can be purchased for money.
They can be made to change sides
With the lure of pelf and power.
I say, they talk of those of us
That have embraced the changes
All around us,
Happily adopted
The mores and manners of the advanced society,
Earned university degrees
That guarantee paying jobs in towns,
Learnt the guile and artfulness of electoral politics,
And are now rebooted with new soft skills
That will ensure functionality in a modern world—
Their hardware old and yet intact.
They can change colours like the chameleons
Or like the proverbial bat, switch sides with ease.
But tribals never yield the ground.
They never change.
Change is something we dread.
We cannot change—they say—
We must be made to change—
We must learn to conform—
We must be educated—
We must be made to wear the Western garbs
As it is unsightly to see people running naked around
trees
Like the beasts in the jungle.
In the enlightened and civilized world,
No one should remain backward and underdeveloped.
Let us bring progress to them—they say—

Let us build towns and cities for them
So that they become shopkeepers, tradesmen,
Politicians, and bureaucrats—
Not some hunters and gatherers
Who dabble with bows and arrows
And other crude metal weapons.
Let us clear the thick forest,
Get rid of all the animals living in there for safety
reasons.
They must be taught that
The trees, rivers, and the mountains are priceless
But have to be cleaved, deforested, and dammed
In order to make more resources
For development and progress—for civilization.
Let us change the tribals for their own sake.
In the process, they stereotype us
And brand us with names,
Treat us as like second-class citizens in our own
country.
Just because we are tribals
And we somehow refuse to change
Or yield to all their unjust demands.

ON LEAVING THE VILLAGE

I left for a Salesian school early in life,
Eager for some sort of education.
I was not the lone pioneer in the field;
Before me
The older boys
Had trundled down the slope of our hills
To the plains
Where these schools
That took catechism classes were built,
Off the inner line[1]
Forbidden to enter
The restricted areas peopled with quaint tribes
Living in protective isolation of the government.
And after me, younger boys
In droves were put to these same schools
Where all of us acquired,
Apart from many other important things,
Two of the most empowering tools for life,
Hindi and English —
One was the so-called national language of India
And the other, tongue of the rich and famous.

---

1   The inner line regulation of 1878, which prohibited outsiders
    from entering the North East Frontier Agency, later christened as
    Arunachal Pradesh in 1972.

The heady cocktail of the two
Implied a ticket to wealth and happiness.
Our well-meaning folks were anxious
That we learn the ways of the clever *Hariangs*[1] —
Their ABC and their 123
(Which we learnt by rote with dexterity);
Their songs and dances, their religion,
And learnt to see people and places, ourselves included,
From their perspectives;
We even learnt to acquire for ourselves
The trappings of a gentleman in their society,
Learnt to smoke and gamble, booze and party,
Ride a desk, drive a car, sing a Bollywood song,
Contest election, bid for tender works,
Climb up the social ladder,
Socialize and hobnob with VIPs in the corridors of
power,
All these and everything else
That made them the more civilized than us
We learned
That we forgot everything about ourselves,
Our customs, our traditions, our history, our world
view.
Now after us,
Our children have disowned their mother tongue
And smirk at our piety brazenly.
I left my village,
And many years later,

---

1   Meaning non-tribals in Nyishi dialect.

A man came back,
Clueless and nonchalant,
In place of the boy who was long gone.
The boy was like the river for whom
Returning was never an option —
To its amniotic source —
Rolling back the years —
Halting the clock's hands—
Defying the *Donyi-Polo*.[1]
The broken man had nothing to salvage
From the wreckage of empty homes,
Only faded memories of times gone by
That seem to have little to do with me.

---

1   The sun and moon.

My Brother, You Live in the City

I don't understand most of what you say —
You speak a different language now.
You put on strange clothes,
And your mannerisms, they are stranger!
It is quite unlike the man I used to know
From the man I meet now after so many years.
You are like the intrepid explorer
Who has come to see my world now —
To seek adventure and thrill.
A spelunker
Of the chthonic underbellies of our primitive life.
An anthropologist
For whom tribes living with cultures intact
Are good museum specimens.
Or might you be a pen friend
Whom I never met but wrote to me nonetheless —
Just for the heck of it.
Your desire to know the ways of the *Nyipak*,[1]
Your keenness to be one of them,
Your selfishness, your ego, your enterprising nature,
Your one-upmanship

---

1   Another word for non-tribal or outsiders in Nyishi.

Has taken you far away from our village,
From the people who know you,
From me, who suckled of the same mother as you.
My brother, you live in the city
Where they say men are taught to scorn their culture
And women made to spurn their lovers,
Where little children are taught to lisp foreign words
And feel ashamed of their mother tongue.
Look how you lord over us now,
Basking in your newfound glory,
Your arrogance and knowledge
That you have finally outwitted me
In wealth, in power,
And in that thing that you call education,
Which I take to be some odious and loathsome,
Dangerous weapon of self-annihilation.

TOMORROW

I am from somewhere
Where there is no tomorrow
For our children.
The last leaf has fallen
From the tree
In the land I come from.
In the land I come from,
No respite seems in sight
For the poor of the earth,
For the unemployed youth,
For the wretched mother of the child
Who will grow up to spurn his own people,
For the rivers diverted from their course,
For the mountains split of their innards,
For the forest whose resources are plundered
In the name of some ubiquitous developments,
Ironically the 'tomorrow'
Awaiting us with open arms.
Tomorrow
Is not for people who cannot read and write.
Tomorrow
Is not for people who are threatened with extinction.
Tomorrow
Is not for the weak and helpless.

The 'tomorrow' (if any, for us)
Will be there to merely deceive us,
Again and again,
Like the wily politician with a forked tongue,
Selling to us the vision of a better life.
We have bartered our today
And lost our past
—At a great cost of everything else with us —
Only for this damn thing called tomorrow
Which we do not know if it exists at all for us.

A DIRGE FROM THE NORTH-EAST

The book of maps
Says nothing about our lands and forest rights,
The exploitation of the poor by the rich,
The loss of our traditions and culture,
Disease, death, and hunger:
A book of wry infographics,
Its intricate lines and legends are the tools
Used by the spin doctors
To manufacture a new myth for us every day.
Our school day's pledge reinforcing
What the book of maps tries to teach us
And others of our ilk:
All Indians are our brothers and sisters.
It never tried to tell us that
We are the proud children of *Abotani*.[1]
The fallout was that
We took to wearing curious Western garbs
Convinced that the old feathers were shed,
So that bright, new ones would grow in their place.
We happily adopted strange customs and habits

---

1   The mythical forefather of the Tani group of tribes, Nyishi, Adi,
Apatani, Galo, and Mishings of Assam.

Without any foresight.
We began using strange speeches
To commune with one other.
We developed a stranger compulsion
To be accepted and to be endorsed by the other.
Thus overwhelmed
By our self-indulgences,
Our endless appetite for the new wealth,
Our newfound lust for life—that had us dazed,
The tribes sail under the banner of new gods
In search of new beginnings.
But no one knows why
When the vessels were put to the sea
We drifted away from one other,
In different directions,
To different shores—
Victims of stochastic events,
We seek refuge in a delusionary future—
That looks more comforting than the past,
Through all our wonderings,
Through all the routes taken by our forbearers
To reach the present
We call our beloved homeland.
The trespassers, not knowing what to call the place,
Named it, in alien tongue, Arunachal Pradesh,
Albeit the land of rising sun.
Impressive, *Nee?*
Reminds us of a great country in the Far East,
In the heart of the Pacific,
Well known for its advancement

In scientific civilization.
They even rechristened our lakes,
Our rivers, our forests, our institutions,
Our men, women, and children
After their own names of places and faces.
That is how the 'Gekar Sinyi'[1] became the 'Ganga'[2]—
Maybe to purify the brackish waters
Saturated with innocent tribal superstitions.
That is how we have a surfeit of institutions
Named after this great Indian leader
And that patriotic Indian freedom fighter.
And that is how my cousin is named
After a famous Bollywood star.
Giving names to our lands and its people
Is no longer our prerogatives,
In our Swaraj.
This land
Where our ancestors lie buried
Is a no man's land for the interlopers,
Who believe that anyone can intrude into
And lay claim on the rivers, mountains, and trees
By putting a tag on them.
Of course, you don't notice these things at the first.
People accustomed to seeing
The glitz and glamour of city life
Are the least bothered about a mere fob
In the backwaters of civilization.

---

1   Name of a local lake near Itanagar, the state capital of Arunachal Pradesh and popularly known as the Ganga Lake.

2   Name of a major Indian river.

There is nothing to covet here,
No wealth, no pomp or personal glory;
Only the harsh realities of life—
The everyday business of living and dying.
Who would want such stuff?
Who would want to know such a place?
Not famous like Bangalore,
Known for its aeronautical industry,
Tinseltown Mumbai, Metro Kolkata,
Madras—oops! Chennai, is it?
Or for instance, Michael Jackson's America.
We Indians have a strange habit of talking
About Bill Gates or Madhuri Dixit
As if they are just next-door neighbours
With whom we exchange pleasantries every day.
Our knowledge
Of the rich and famous is so minute
That we know
When one of those celebrity couples
Had a fight over a piece of toothpick
In one of the many socialite evenings,
To the lurid particularities
Of their undergarments' colour
And their innumerable fads and fetishes.
Yet you would not know
Where my home state is
Or pretend not to know
Just in order to put us to size.
That way you let us know our equations—
Our place under the sun—

When you mistake us
For a Japanese or a Chinese tourist.
You know so little about us,
Despite six decades of living together
And adopting your freedom fighters
As our patriots,
Accepting your government,
Learning to speak your languages,
And trying to fit in every possible way.
And then you exhort us to join the mainstream
Whenever someone amongst us
Goes astray (as you say).
I need a clarification here:
What is this mainstream that you talk about often?
Is it a big stream
Where all the tributaries lose their identities?
Where the smaller fishes live
In perpetual fear of the bigger fishes
In a fish eat fish world?

WHO ARE WE?

Who are we?
We are tribal people
Living in north-east India.
We are a group of 26 major tribes
And more than hundred and ten sub-tribes
Living in the land of our ancestors;
Where the tricolour flies now with impunity;
Where development has come—
Education, health service, and social welfare measures,
Employment opportunities, new technology,
New religions competing to harvest our souls,
New age assumptions on these matters and the art of
living,
New cars and vehicles, new drugs and psychotropic
substances
For our sons and daughters,
New music from Bollywood,
And all the louder music from DJ parties
And rock music festivals
(New sounds for our ears, indeed)—
Many of the new things are gifted to us
By our benevolent masters.
Many are also thrust upon us
And we accept them without a protest,

Believing that fate has decreed it:
An unchanging and unbending fate that
Made us lose control over our own destiny.

Who are we?
We live in Arunachal Pradesh,
A state in the Indian union.
And we have learnt to call ourselves *Arunachalee,*
As if we are a group of nameless and homeless tribe,
A new specimen of mankind
That our benevolent masters located in the subtropical jungle
Promptly coining a new name to own it—
A genus of the species *Homo Arunachalsis.*
We used to call ourselves Galo,[1] Nyishi,[2] Apatani[3]
And we used to have beautiful names
For every patch of the forest,
Every stone, stream, river, hill, and mountain.
Wherever our ancestors have hunted and trodden,
Those places have faces and identities.
They are an extension of us.
They are the larger system of our biological community.
They are in our songs and dances,
In the patterns that our womenfolk weave on clothes,

---

1   The tribe inhabiting West Siang, parts of East Siang, and Upper Subansiri district of the state.

2   The tribe inhabiting Papumpare, Lower Subansiri, Kurung Kumey, Kra Dadi, East Kameng, and parts of Upper Subansiri district of the state.

3   The tribe inhabiting Lower Subansiri district of the state.

Conspicuously present in our food habits and simple
lifestyle.
Now known as Arunachal Pradesh
And made part of the Indian union,
The streams, the rivers, the forests, and the mountains
Are also claimed by the red dragon.
They came in 1962[1] and told us:
'Look at us . . . how we look like you.
You are chinks like us, my dear brothers.
We are here only to drive away
The brown and hairy people off your property.'
So here we are, also the subject of international
diplomacy,
A bone of contention between two Asian giants
Striving to dominate each other in the subcontinent.

Who are we?
We were the worshippers of our ancestors,
The almighty sun and moon;
But now our people are signing up
To join the armies of Allah, Jesus, and Ram.
We are also the people who have lost
The ability to speak our own mother tongue.
Our children now speak Hindi and English
To go to the university
And secure good jobs for themselves.
We are not known much in our own country,

---

1   China invaded India through Ladakh and Arunachal Pradesh (then
     North Eastern Frontier Agency) in 1962.

As the rest of India mistake us
For a Chinese, a Korean, or a Japanese.
We live in a very underdeveloped part of the country.
We are ever dependent on centrally sponsored schemes.
Here we would like to add
That we are poor but our land is rich.
Our boys and girls have talent but lack opportunities.
Ambition and willpower dissipates
In the face of condescension, stigma,
And the right connection in the corridors of power.
At home our leaders with their glib tongue misguide us.
They sell our rivers to the power developers.
They lease out our forests to the saw millers.
They privatize our personal needs
And syndicate every bit of our common interests.
They corporatize our institutions
Along with our emotions and feelings.
They mortgage our future for their immediate gains.
We are mere cannon fodders
To their larger game plan in political one-upmanship.
Brought up in these circumstances,
Do we have any particular world view?
In fact, we are yet to figure out where we stand
In the pantheon of the great races of mankind.
We have no time to look at the world
Beyond these mountain walls that circumscribe us
And shield us.
Our pressing problems back at home
Call for immediate solutions.
So this is how we would like to introduce

Ourselves to the world
That is the least bothered about us
And all the others of our ilk
Busy as it is always with feting the likes of Mr Obama
And dealing with the ISIS and Boko Haram in the
West.
But now and then, even we ask this of ourselves:
Who are we?

A Trophy Poem

What gossamer dreams are spun on your loin
looms with deft fingers working adroitly like the
Arachnid masters of your art? The geometrical
contours leap joyfully and sing brazenly of
Undulating peaks rising up to kiss multi-hued
skies and meandering rivers falling off
The edges of its finite space. As lines morph
into the sun, moon and stars across
Time, cowries, Tibetan bell metals, household
trinkets, trees, flowers, myths,
And Märchen mutate into strange
hieroglyphic and begin to speak in
Tongues . . . Words then align themselves
into the shape of a trophy,
A coveted trophy poem, when Nyishi weavers inspire! A
Tapestry of copious forms and warm colours running
Riot all over its beautiful canvas! May *Jiwt*,[1]
Beloved mother goddess, who taught you
The art form, bless your tribe to grow.
May the rainbow in the sky presage good omen

---

1   The daughter of the sun goddess, who was married to Abotani, the
    mythological Adam-like figure of the Tani group of tribes, from
    whom it is believed that the tribes learnt the art of loin loom weaving
    as also from the spiders.

For you after every spell of the rain. May the fowls with
Their bright plumages roost in your dreams.
May the fibrous nettles, the wild
Orchids, and the spawns of dye plants growing
in the depth of your forests thrive
To prosper like you. But in the wake of
automation and the onslaught of cheaper bazaar
Goods, your daughters today do not have
the time or the knack for a dying art ...
And you should know better!

IGUANA

In the heart of a city,
A cluster of bamboos and few trees
Throb with life.
The ganglion of vegetal remains
Had been spared for the time being only
By the sprawls of the urban growth
With their innocuous smoking habits.
In the heart of the city,
Nay, inside its very core
Where its aspic tissues are pristine,
Yet to be singed by the fumes
Emitting from dyspeptic factories and its sick people
Or sullied by the filth and grimes
From the numerous chock-a-block sewers and canals,
There an iguana has a home for itself
Burrowed deep into the moist earth
Safe from the heats of the sweltering city,
As the birds of the air drop by
Looking for food and shelter amongst its foliage,
Thriving for the moment
Because the landlord had no money to develop the
property
As of then, perhaps.
Last heard, a real estate guy purchased the plot

After paying through his nose.
But before that,
The patch of green forest
Already had swarms of slum-boys
Scouring through its thick undergrowth
For small games and wild berries.
One of the wretched souls
Smashed the brittle head of a sunbird.
He later boasted about it to his friends—
That what a good shot he was with the catapult.
The silent cove with ancient eyes
Witnessed more acts of blood and gore
Following that act which took an avian life.
The iguana too had been pulled out of its hole
And taken away
Despite some muffled protest
Which only the trees heard,
Brooding under the grey sky of the March month
And having seen it all
Made a foregone conclusion about themselves too . . .

I WILL TELL YOU WHY
WE ARE ANGRY

I will tell you why we are angry.
It is because you never asked of us
What exactly is that we want from you civilized fellows.
You came and said that this will be good for us
And we believed you.
I will tell you why we are so scared.
It is because our own children now disown us.
They do not believe in the old tales of the tribe
And prefer to believe in all that you say,
Through your newspapers, magazines, cinema, the TV,
And the Internet,
Through the mediums of your pop songs, rock songs,
Hip hop, Hollywood, and Bollywood;
They lure and show them a way
That is full of pitfalls and tragedies if they are not very
careful.
I will tell you why some of them have started to take
drugs.
It is because they have forgotten the old ways.
They are schooled and educated
And need not seek out an old man for a tip
On the art of living.

They don't know that life is meant to be happy
And happiness can never be bought by money or
power.
I will tell you why some of them have started to steal
and take up guns.
It is because most of them are unemployed and poor,
Desperate and in need of help.

To Our Benevolent Masters

Benevolent masters!
You had masters before
You developed the capability
To become a master yourself—
Of our people and our land—
Our forest and mineral resources.
How does it feel to be lorded over by foreigners?
Know that the feeling is very mutual here.
They came in the guise of traders
And captured your sea ports
And destroyed your impregnable forts,
Took over your cities and towns
And educated you in Macaulay's English
So that you could be clerks
And confidant of the empire.
It took some time for you to realize
That the empire had nothing to offer you.
In fact, it was evil and debased you.
So you threw off its yoke from your shoulders.
Now that you are a master yourself
I need to ask you
If the past has taught you anything.

You came to us as our saviour,
To teach our people new knowledge.
You brought us new technology,
Very much like the *firangis*[1]
Who brought the railways
And the telegraph to you.
You were benevolent and kind
And had us really falling for your words
Of hope in the future
Among the nation of your people.
Allow us to be there.
Give us time and the space that we need
So that we can stand proudly hand in hand
And march towards peace and progress
Together.
Do not let yourself be deluded
That any race of people can be taken for granted
Or that history is linear
Remember what the son of God had said,
'The first will be last and the last will be first'.
You of all people,
Benevolent masters,
Should know that slavery and apartheid
Have long ago disappeared in Africa and America.
You should treat your countrymen
With equal respect and dignity.
Our girls are not safe in your capital city.
Our teenaged sons are lynched

---

1   Meaning 'foreigners' in Hindi.

In your streets by mobs.
You say we are Indians;
Show us how an Indian
Should treat another Indian.
Show us your great dharma and ahimsa.
Show to mankind
That the whole world is a global village.

When an Indian from the Mainland Is Knifed in Australia

When an Indian from the mainland is knifed in Australia,
They talk about it on the TV and newspapers,
Condemning the dastardly behaviour of the assailants.
The prime minister writes to his counterpart in Sydney,
Protesting in his strongest terms.
Mr Ambassador is then summoned.
A major diplomacy row erupts.
If it is a man from the mainland, our people say,
There are strikes, hartals, and more debates on TV
And more newspaper coverage.
Together the nation
Puts its whole weight behind the victim and his family.
And everyone screams in chorus:
Inhumane, savagery, or murder most foul!
The country is ready to go to war also—
If the man is from mainland India, our people say.

But when a fellow Indian from the north-east is mugged
Or beaten to death in the streets
Of Delhi, Pune, and Bangalore city,
Why is the rest of India so silent?

Where has the prime minister gone?
Where are the TV and newspapers
Who gloss it over
For the more sensational news of the day?
And in the process
Our brothers Nido Tania[1] and Richard Loitham[2]
Our sister Ramchanpy Hongray[3]
Add up to the body count only—
Statistical figures—
Along with all the other victims
Of intolerance and hatred
In the country
That was built on the lofty ideals
Of liberty, equality, and fraternity.
In the land
That is sovereign, socialist, democratic, republic.

As north-east bleed,
The rest of India is bland and heartless.
It makes no sense
To distinguish north-east

---

1   Nido Tania, a twenty-year-old student from Arunachal Pradesh (in
    north-east India) was murdered in Lajpat Nagar, New Delhi, in 29
    January 2014 by a group of people who had previously made racist
    comments against him, triggering widespread protests.

2   Richard Loitham, a nineteen-year-old student from Manipur (also in
    the north-east India) was found dead in his hostel room in Bangalore
    in 17 April 2012, and his friends and family had alleged that he had
    died as a consequence of an assault by his seniors.

3   Ramchanphy Hongray, a young Naga girl of nineteen years of age
    from Manipur (also in the north-east India) was murdered in Munirka
    on 24 October 2009 by one IIT-Delhi PhD scholar.

From the rest of India.
In the land where people celebrate diversity—
In the land where the sages proclaim
That the world is a global village—
In the land of satya and ahimsa—
In the land of the Mahatma and Buddha—
In the land where the people venerate
The pir and the baba equally,
There cannot be intolerance and hatred—
There cannot be malice or prejudice.
Man from the mainland India,
We seek an answer.

WILL I HEAR THE JEW'S HARP AGAIN?

Will I hear the Jew's harp again
Amidst the green jhum fields
Up in the mountains,
Under the canopy
Of the open blue sky?
Feeling the sensation
Of freedom and pleasure
Course through my being
Like the rivers entering Assam
To feed her floodplains.
That was a long time ago.
Today,
Not many know
That the Jew's harp
Also belonged to our people—
Simple musicians
With limited repertoire
But with music that ripped off your soul.
It has been replaced
With the drums and guitar, the keyboards,
Experimental sounds from music software,
Sounding the death knell

To all the blessed experience
Of playing the Jew's harp
In the open sky
Amidst the green stalks of paddy
On a breezy afternoon
Up in the mountains.

Will I hear the reed pipes again
In the twilight
When the village folks are back
In their homes
From their fields up in the mountains?
When the kitchen fires are aglow
And smoke rise from the longhouses
To the sky.
When the heartbroken lover
Pours out his grief
To the neighbourhood
And the plaintive number
Numbs all who hear of it.
That was a pretty long time ago.
The longhouses have been pulled down
And the villages emptied out,
As the people have left for the cities
In search of better days.

Will I hear my grandpa recount to me
All my boyhood stories
Once more
As he used to

By the fireside?
I could smell his dirty clothes
Which reeked of smokes and tobacco leaves.
That was a long, long time ago
My grandpa is gone now,
And this generation
Would choke at his scent
And berate him for his poor personal hygiene.
This generation
Hardly remembers its own stories
And sadly the children have given up
Speaking their own language.

I recall the days
When we were free men
Without the anxieties and doubts of civilization
And the strict rules and regimen
Of the civilized fellow
With his clock and dates,
His laws and prison walls,
His social etiquettes,
And his suffocating religion.
I still recall the indolent days
That mollycoddled us
And spoilt us,
Tied us to our mother's apron strings,
Never letting us grow up really.

1962

They came from the mountains
And also from the plains—
Soldiers yellow, brown, and black—
And murdered one other
In our backyard.
Who were they?
Why did they come?
What were they doing in our lands?
No one amongst us had the slightest clue.
But they came in swarms
And fought each other
With weapons that could shoot down the stars
And shake the whole earth,
That frightened us
And made us scamper deeper into the forest for cover.
Each side claimed the victory for himself.
But now we know
Why they bloodied one another's noses,
Why they betrayed one another,
Even as their leaders shook hands
With a smile on their faces

Saying: 'Indi-Chini bhai bhai.'[1]
Now we know why they renegaded on one another,
Backslapping and then backstabbing one another.
Now we realized
That it was to have a mastery over us,
To claim our lands and its resources,
To increase the size of their maps
For strategic considerations,
For ambition and hubris,
Not out of concern for our language and culture
Or for us, the children of the dawn.
Two of the world's oldest civilizations
Clashing like idiots,
Like brutes,
For the spoils of war.

---

1 'Indi-Chini bhai bhai' was a catchphrase of India's diplomacy with
   China in the 1950s, meaning 'India and China are brothers'.

I Knew of a Place in the Mountains

It isn't the great big pleasures that count the most;
It's making a great deal out of the little ones.
—Jean Webster

I knew of a place in the mountains,
A small town
Of few hundred men and women
Who knew each other so well
Like they had been together for ages
Under one roof.
Nearby, a small stream emptied itself into a big river
Furiously rushing down the valley
And the sierra of bulky mountains
Girdling the town
Trying to trap the river
Within its strong walls;
So that nothing escaped from there—
Every little sight and sound,
The people and their memories,
Their songs and their prayers,
The stories birthed by them
Which bespoke of courtship and heartbreak,

Death and dignity,
Pride and honour,
Among clansmen of the tribes,
The aura of the whole town
Peopled with *Wiyus.*[1]
I was ebullient and full of pluck
Living in the midst
Of these immortal people
In a queer little town up in the mountains.
It was also the time
When life's simple pleasures
Brought so much happiness to me.
For instance,
In the sunrise and sunset,
In flowers and in plants,
The birds of the air
And the beasts of the forest,
In the first snow of the season,
In the friendly chit-chats with my neighbours
In the courtyard of the house
On matters that were never scholarly and learned
But concerning ourselves—
About some wedding in the family,
A deadly sore on the calf's leg
After the heifer had died the night before
After she fell from a height,
About the locusts that ravaged the jhum fields,
About the doctor who was newly arrived,

---

1   Meaning 'spirits' in Nyishi.

About the fallen woman who had eloped with an
army man,
The son who had left for a boarding school,
The handsome Catholic priest who was baptizing
people,
The new items sold in the markets by the traders,
The black-and-white cinemas and their songs,
The neighbour's son who had become a dandy
And a fashion plate.
Back then people had plenty of time
And enjoyed one another's company.
They were spontaneous and without frills.
The town was new
And was filled with migrants and arrivistes
From villages and other towns far away,
Tribal and non-tribal,
All looking for a better life.
Everything was easy
And not so screwed up as today.
It had wooden houses with louvred planks
Along with tribal longhouses on their stilts,
The tiny temple where people went to pray
To Hindu gods without unease,
The market, the primary health centre,
The school, and the tricolour that flew high on the
mast
For everyone to fear and respect.

I knew of such a town in the mountains.
A place never visited by you.

A time never experienced by you.
No road will take you there now
Because the old footpath
Has been discarded
In favour of the wide modern roads
Where vehicles can ply.
The new road will not take you there.
It cannot go there
Because it is not the same town in the mountains
That I knew.
It has changed into a nasty place
Inhabited by selfish and insensitive souls
Who do not have time for one another,
Who are busy making money
And chasing impossible goals in life.
It is not the town where the majority takes pride
In speaking their mother tongue.
It is not the town where children look up to the night
sky
And marvel at the stars in their infinite numbers.
It is not the town where they go for a swim
Because the river is too polluted and dirty.
It is not the place covered with snow
As the jungles have been felled for the sake of
development
And the weather is warm and solicitous.
The place I knew of in the mountains
Is long gone now.
In its place, a new township has come up
With tall concrete buildings and sophisticated lifestyle.

Where the feeling of hopefulness
Has given way to bitterness and contempt.
Where the momentous journey
From solitude to loneliness is intuitive and prompt.
Where laughter is always tinged with sadness
At the thought of gaining so little
At the cost of so much,
And that too without any guarantee.
Where crooked modern ideas teach you
To buy and sell love like a commodity
And ride roughshod over people's feelings.
Where the people are not sentimental fools
And therefore need not know
Their neighbours intimately,
The names of the birds and animals
That live in their forest—
They are not very important
To a hip and modern man today.
In fact, the skills that you learn today
Should help you to
Unlearn the past
Like discarding the restraining coils of a cocoon
To fly away to an exciting future.
You forget the past and look to the future only.
In the new town that you know of,
There is science and technology,
Culture and civilization,
Politics and pornography,
So much party and fun,
But then there is no place for the people whom I knew of

And who used to live in the town
Where your parents lived too.
The old town carried the weight of their expectations
for too long
And sank into oblivion
Taking into the depth of its lair
Their old way of living and dying,
Singing and dancing.

MORE VIGNETTES

The clouds, like speech bubbles, hanging over the
silhouette of distant mountains
Talk to me of people looking for lost pride along the
banks of an ancient river—
Sifting among gold dust, sand grains, pebbles, rocks for
a forgotten moment of their history.
The river has as an old tale to tell too;
Of dream children making sand sculptures of forgotten
landscape and faces of people whose names hardly
matter now
And the breaking tides licking old memories, like the
mother of a young calf.
In the lap of Siang[1] the foreigners seeking more adventures
In their extravagance unwittingly exorcised the ghosts
of our forefathers
Who had been living with us, undying, for ages as
tutelary spirits.
The grey heads then trail-blazed the road to Eden

---

1   The Siang is one of the major rivers of Arunachal Pradesh and a
      tributary of the Brahmaputra. The Adi tribesmen living in and around
      Pasighat area located on the bank of river Siang were one of the first
      people from the region to come in contact with the Britishers as
      they aggressively pushed forward to the foothills of the North East
      Frontier areas for tea plantation.

Where some of us learnt alien tongues
And acquired exotic habits that made us forget ourselves.

II

The river's heart is older than the folds of the white
Kuradadi.[1]
It feels the gentle throb of life that pulsates in the heart
of lovers.
And I, like the inhabitant of an ancient city,
Thirst for a drop from its amniotic source
Which is a regular haunt for my herd
And where my master comes to lead me salt-licking[2] home.
The river had a voice too.
Now smothered and noiseless.
Its voice lost to the light of the day.
The night is empty too.
I have strained to hear the voice I heard in my childhood
In the raucous music of the valley and in its cold drifts too
I have strained to trace lost notes of the eloping river
Kurung.[3]
A mere shadow of shadows,
The old hag visited me in a dream.

---

1 Kuradadi is the local name for Himalayan range in Nyishi dialect.

2 It refers to the practice of offering the Mithun (Bos frontalis) salt on
   the palm of the hand and enticing it to come close to the owner who
   can then noose it with a lariat.

3 Legend has it that the river Kurung eloped with her lover and failed
   to secure her parent's blessings, who in turn cursed and threw ashes
   from the hearth after her. As a result, it is believed that her waters are
   perennially soiled and murky to this day.

III

The sunrays light up the face of distant mountains—
On a dull afternoon, as usual, vehicles ply the streets
honking loudly—
Men come and go like termites crawling all over a
molehill.
While in a room of a city hotel, a conference is
underway
Where people are discussing feverishly about rights,
Conspiring to call a strike—to burn a bus, loot
properties, and cause mayhem,
In support of a charter of demands ignoring duties . . .
Men like termites—termites in a molehill—
Vehicles honking in the street on a dull afternoon—
Sunrays on the face of a mountain that is russet
bracken.

IV

In the evening;
The whistles and catcalls of roadside Romeos and
delinquents;
The blare of the soundbox from a lecherous audio
system;
Painted girls in body-hugging clothes and short skirts
Insinuating the size, shape, and colour of their pallid
bums and shapely torsos.
It is scandalous to see them among gape-mouthed
commuters, pan sellers,
And moustached vendors

Having the boner moments and giddiness of a frenetic
river
On the brink of ravaging the land with rapacious
deluges.

V

Yet the need remains to love someone—find love.
Perhaps, it is inherent like our instinct for survival
Even in an age marked by suicidal tendencies
With friends turning to foes
And neighbours threatening to nuke you.
You spell out a clear nuclear doctrine
Of a credible minimum deterrence,
Of the capability to retaliate and inflict harm
To someone who dares to moisten your eye
And makes you cringe in the face of intimidations
Or for some act of infidelity.
The river's liquid wisdom seeps
Through chinks that make our gullibility culpable.

THE UPSTART

He was an old acquaintance
From the part of town that is our skid row,
Where less-fortunate souls
Fought each other for slops and space
And also with their own quirky fates.
I still visualize him walking down the streets
Of our locality, tall, gaunt, and angry,
Scuffing a torn slipper on the tarmac.
That was seven years ago.

But yesterday when I met him in the market square,
I noticed that he had put on weight
And was in designer wears,
Flashing a wicked smile on his now portly face,
Brimming with confidence and elan
Coming in the wake of stability and wealth.
'My god! How you have changed overnight,'
(He barely heard it)—as I said to myself.

He was very kind enough to me though
As we tried to catch up with each other
After a gap of so many years.
So we talked about the small secrets
We shared during those days of our struggle.

Every little trespass that often got us,
The squatters,
On the wrong side of the law.
Our endless days of privation and defeat.

Then he announced to me,
'I would like to do something for you—
I mean it—you see, I have lots of money now.'
But somehow I could already see through his little
game
As a small crowd gathered around the scene of our
union.
It seems even as he addressed me,
He was speaking to the passersby,
Some of them who knew him as the man
Who gave lots of donations to charitable organizations,
A pukka philanthropist who liked to help the poor,
A budding politician who vouched for changes
In the way political parties run
And talked about inner party democracy
And God knows what other political jargons
That he threw about here and there
Which a humble man from the street like me
Cannot really make out.

So here he was, ready to help me,
A writer in indigent circumstance.
I wondered how.
'I can give you anything,' he declared with the air of
finality.

'Anything?' I quizzed.
He thought I was too poor to comprehend riches.
But he balked
When I begged of him the virtuosity of Turner's
painting,
The imaginative depth of Dali's art,
The range and finish of Shakespearean drama,
The profundity of Einstein's mind,
The love and humanity of Gandhi,
Patriotism of Bhagat Singh.

And I added: 'Sir, since you are so influential,
Put in a few words to the Almighty to give me
The compassion of Christ,
The divinity of Buddha,
And the creativity of Brahma.'

JOURNEY TO TIBET

(Loosely based on a Nyishi folktale)

'Sister, oh sister! Our parents are too old to fend for
themselves.
Therefore, look after home and hearth;
While we, your two brothers, cross the land of snow to
Tibet.'

'Brothers, oh my brothers, no,' said a dimpled lass,
Scouring for her outfits in the scant light of the hearth's
fire
Licking its tongue in some bovine foresight—
'The beauty of the snow-capped mountains
beckons me.
Moreover, from the land of Lamas
Some soul, a friend from the past life maybe, longs
for me.
My heart throbs and my feet dance to the measure of
his hoot.'

'Sister, our sweet sister, your hands are limp,
Your foot too tender to stomp and crawl over ice and
stones,
Your brittle lips will crackle

From the whip lashed in abandon by the chilly winds,
Your pretty face will lose its charm
Scourged by the hazards of our enterprise.'

'Brothers, my brothers, though the journey be full of
perils,
Though I may never return to see our poor parents—
As uncertainties assail our beaten tracks,
Though be smothered in a snowstorm
Or dropped down dead a precipice,
Though be cast under the spell
Of the tutelary spirits in the alpine heights
Or at the mortal hands of an enemy I meet my fate—
Yet perish I will with the twinkle of a dream in my eyes
And a swansong on my lips.
Mistake not my grace and beauty for frailty.
Though be of the weaker sex,
My body is lithe and my spirit brave
To face any hazards of your enterprise.'

Thus, incessantly pleaded
The doe-eyed beauty to her older siblings,
Unwilling to tag along
An extra piece of burden to slacken their pace.
Their old parents shook heads at their headstrong
daughter.
Thinking what lay in store for her in the future.
A child given to odd whimsies and fancies,
Violent tantrums and passions,
She was a far cry from the coy and homely woman

They craved for from the almighty *Donyi-Polo*.

'Stay, stay home with us, child,' the grey heads pleaded;
'In the wintry landscapes of the *Kuradadi*
The waters of the lake come to life
Pulling unsuspecting sojourners to their stygian graves,
The arms of the air cart off people
Beyond the singularity of time and space
Where you will be homeless and nameless—
Lost you will be to us, oh precious daughter.'
The lipoid words of wisdom dripped down
The hissing flame that darted up to fang
Layers of adipose tissue smoking above the hearth.

Morning was bathed in the alpenglow of dawn.
Darkness was gone.
Mist had cleared away.
Then, two brothers set forth
For the *Nyime Nyoku*[1] without their sulking sister.
They descended a valley,
Forded a stream, and climbed a mountain,
But the horizon ran away.
And when they had descended another valley,
Forded another stream to climb another mountain
With the horizon still running away,
It had been days since their kid sister had left home
Trailing them like the lengthening shadows of dusk.
The brothers lured her

---

1   *Nyime Nyoku*—local name in Nyishi for the Tibetan plateau.

With promises of warm clothes, beads, bell metals,
And other paraphernalia from the Tibetan bazaar
To return home.
They coaxed, cajoled, and cuffed her,
But she stood blandly immune to all posturings.

All along the way, she sang with the birds
And lisped to the warble of the brook,
Blushed at the wind's coquetry
And flirted unabashedly with the sparkle of the
sunlight
On dewdrops and on the snowy peaks.
The drudgery of her household chores left behind,
She caterwauled in delight
As the four directions stood enchanted
Blessing this happy child in their encumbrances—
Alas! How swiftly time flies for a happy person—
Alas! How one is made to suffer excesses
Committed in the heat of short exciting moments—

In her exuberance, she threw to the four winds the
taboos
Passing through bewitched grounds.
She also forgot to throw a morsel from her victuals
At the presiding deities of the forest as rituals.
She forgot not to sing loudly
And not to dance deliriously;
Nor to cast her lingering looks
At the frigid lakes and the stark beauty of the
whitescape;

She forgot not to whistle and clap her hands in delight
At such unexpected beauty and freedom.
And at the same time, she plucked a bunch of wild
orchids
That had never been seen by her before in life.
The roots of the orchid tree began to clasp her sylphid
frame
For no human hands had dared to bear away its
blossoms before.
She tried to shake it off, but the roots kept coiling
around her
Like Hydra-headed serpents.
Panic-stricken, she called out
To her two kindreds oblivious to her plight.
'Brothers, oh my dear brothers,
Strange vines bind my hands and restrain my feet.
Pray, unhand these slithering hairs of medusa.
Ah! My viscid flesh snaps drenched of moisture!'

Then two swords commenced to hack
At the stony roots of the cursed tree
Slowly stifling a petrified girl.
In vain the brothers hacked at the roots,
Their swords at hand blunted
Sans the gleam of the light on its blade,
On the dewdrops and on the snowfield
As far as the eye could traverse in that dismal waste

Where the demon *Tamu*[1] devoured the sun.
The vines pressed to breed like a malignant tumour
And swayed their heads in the air
Like the severed heads of the Lernean Hydra
Slowly calcifying a hapless victim
Shrouded in a cloak of stalk and leaves;
So that there remained in the face only
Any semblance to a former spark,
Where a pair of moist eyes rolled in its two sockets
And gritty lips struggled to form words beseeching
succour.

'Brothers, oh my dear brothers, for the love of me,
Make me a bonfire
For I freeze standing motionless for days.
And before you depart, fetch for me dry woods
And stack them as high as these spare mountains
To burn endless winters.

'The advent of spring will add much discomfort to me
As birds of the air will descend to build nests in my clefts,
Peck at my faces with their sharp bills,
And cover all over my craggy features with their faeces.
The archer's weapon will be handy to shoo them
away—
I may even need a few staves too for the wild beasts
That may cross my path.

---

1   *Tamu*—a demon who causes the solar eclipse according to Nyishi
     mythology.

'Dearest brothers, before you leave,
Weed away the bushes and brambles growing around me
For they tickle and annoy endlessly.

'Also leave behind a few pots and pans
To remind me of our mother's culinary arts
And I shall long for the warmth of the fireplace back at
home—
Our Darby and Joan would have then moved on
Without their impish daughter.

'Nay, grieve not at my helplessness,
For blamed will not be you two, my faithful brothers.
My life has been brief and brutal
But I have lived enough to taste pleasure and now this
pain.
I die with a regret that my dream lies unfulfilled . . .
In Tibet, my lover awaits my arrival.'

'Sister! Oh sister! A cold storm approaches
And we lack raiments and viands.
These barren places offer little shelter.
Therefore, we depart for home.
The paths are sealed by the swelling ice and time flies
fast—
To Tibet, another time a sojourn we shall make.
Farewell, thou joy of our ancient house
Whom we have lost to these wildernesses
That may sustain and nourish you in our absence,
perhaps?'

The two brothers retraced their heavy feet homewards,
Descending a valley, fording a stream,
And climbing up a mountain,
Only this time, the horizon raced towards them
As their native village perched on the berm of the
mountain
Appeared nearer and nearer.

Many moons later,
A sojourner to the *Nyime Nyoku*
Happened to stop over a sleepy little hamlet.
He spoke of a giant rock with talismanic power
That could protect passersby in the middle of a foul
place.
He said, 'From afar I saw a beautiful girl
As if beckoning me to come over,
But there stood nothing
Save a huge boulder in her place as I drew nigh.
The whole place was cluttered with rotten twigs and
sticks
Remotely resembling batons, darts, and kinked bows.
I cleared the bushes and brambles
Growing like weeds in great profusion all over the place
And left at the foot of the rock
Some tokens of arrows, bows, and staves.'
A myth was born that instant for some obscure
tribesmen,
Who called themselves the sons of Abotani.

YAI

(Mother)

The moment she was gone,
It dawned on me how much I missed her.
Till then I always took her for granted.
She was just another thing about my life,
Like the gourd vessels, wickerwork baskets,
Bamboo tubes used for filling water,
The moon and the stars in the sky—
Each filling spaces in my private cosmos,
Where even little things had their own use.
And I foolishly thought that we would live on
Un-ageing like the *Wiyus*,
In the exuberance of my youth,
While she cowered in the face of the tall ambitions
And stubbornness of my growing years.
The day was just another ordinary day,
When my mother left me
In the dark,
Not even waiting to say a proper adieu for the last time.
Packing all her clothes and trinkets
Into a big bundle with her cloak—
The very ones soiled by her toils and moils.
She left escorted by strange women

Who exchanged no pleasantries with anyone—
Unseen to all
But visible to the spiritual eyes of the shaman,
Who shouted,
'Oh! She is gone, your mother!
Never to return to the light of the day.'
It was a hasty departure,
Which left me thinking
If the dead lacked courtesy
Or maybe she went away thinking of returning
To her family
As usual
When she rose at the sound of the rooster
Every day in the morning
To leave for her jhum[1] fields
Seven kilometres down the slope of the rugged
mountains.

---

1   The practice of shifting or slash and burn type of agriculture.

The Role Model

The tall bulimic persona is a perfect prop for a designer
wear.
Mascara on twirled eyelashes adds to the charm that is
already there.
The moisturized face and bee-stung pout bleeding
garishly
Is the new look of the Generation X,
Preferring champagnes and cocktails in night parties
To anything old and outdated like folk songs and
meditations,
Prayer service or social works—these are the stuff for
the *Behenji*[1] type.
Further, they like to label beauty as a commodity
Available at a throwaway price,
A soft-selling brand packed for the lure.
You see, ruled by the economics of the glamour world,
There is an endless demand for it over the sales counter
Where buyers haggle with touts as coyness and grace
dies a dog's death
In the flashy boulevards of a socialite's elan and
chutzpah.

---

1   Literal meaning is a respectful term for 'sister' but also used in a
     derogatory manner to denote unfashionable, uncool, housewife sort
     of girls.

In the blinding lights of discotheques and ramps
Where regulated mannequins catwalk,
The feminine mystique is stripteased for voyeurism and
sadistic pleasure.
No more is the little girl willing to be coy and homely
And growing up they aver, 'All these Sati-Savitri[1] stuff
are good to read in the books only.'
At the same time, pointing at a kinkily dressed female
on the cover
Of a tabloid, will say coquettishly, 'She is my role
model.'

---

1   Two examples of virtuous and devoted wife in Indian mythology.

Song of the Driftwoods

Sons of the soil,
Uprooted from homesteads
Along stream-edged habitats of the subtropical forests,
Where a chipmunk flits noisily,
Looking for the familiar mien of a tree he grew up on,
Gorging ripe berries aloft its slender boughs and twigs,
As nearby a group of rhesus monkeys foraged for nits
on their bodies
In an awkward hubbub that belied their buoyancy in
the thin air.

The river had approached them,
As does sly officials unsuspecting tribals
Conjuring up visions of a better tomorrow for them.
It was true: water sustained life, and the river brimmed
with this elixir.

One fateful night, the weather went wild.
It rained hard and lightning flashed like scimitars in the
dark.
'*Leave*,' said the rising tides of the river without much of
a ceremony—
Rivers are known to be spiteful and erratic

And, like politicians, have a poor track record of
redeeming pledges.

Now sticking out of shallows and sandbars
We live like refugees in makeshift tents
In some abandoned constructions of an urban
wasteland.
Marinated by the sun, shower, and rain,
The elements sit on our skins like sleep.
Shorn of our former splendour,
Beggars in our own lands,
We are ever at the mercy of the treacherous river.
'Leave,' the river will ask us gruffly again with the rising
tide,
And once more we will be on the move,
In search of our moorings.

PETER PAN

Mischievous memories
Dance with glee
In the showers of July
Only to be pulled by the ear
And chided to be wary of the cold and cough
The next time it rains
And so every time it rains
On the pretext of visiting an old friend
The little imps come along
To catch up with me
Who has lost track of so many things
And like an insomniac
Can only see the night pass by helplessly
So every time it rains
The hands on the clock fall apart
And for a moment
Everything is yesterday
With the same old rains
Beating down the windswept countryside
And beyond
Over the massive mountain massif
The same old grey sky fat with water
And this loner looking out
At the chiaroscuro of evanescent time

Having grown more grey
But my friends
Like Peter Pan
They just refuse to grow up
Leaving early as they come
But not before parting with the gifts of déjà vu
I am to share with no one
And a promise to return soon
From never-never land.

A REQUIEM FOR THE DEAD

You wound a clockwork toy, it starts to sing or joust.
A mechanical device is programmed to please
And can be assembled or repaired at will too:
But not the mashed skulls, torn tissues, and mangled limbs
Of the dead on the fatal mishap.
The sad relics of beautiful people can no longer talk,
laugh, and cry . . .
And nothing can assuage grieving hearts to bear the loss.
The lifeless mother cannot suckle a limp child in her ghastly hug,
For the brook of life has petered out of her young bosom.
The teenage fashionista in blue denims,
Her face crumpled like a piece of paper,
Is reduced to her deformed self.
Their hearth's fire smothered forever, the young couple
No longer need the warmth of their nuptial bed
Shattered to pieces and strewn all over the silent stream
Like the scrap metals of the bus.
The old man as if looking to finish a gab
Begun before embarking the bus
That took him to the nook of death.

How violent, short, and brutish is man's life sometimes!
Given to all the vagaries of fortune and misfortune,
How futile his ambitions and vanities!
Here is a schoolboy thrust up the slope in his wet
uniform.
They cut out the crap, but he had the last laugh, I guess.
Now lost is he to the world forever.
Whose child? Did his mother cry?
Or the tears simply refused to fall from its height?
Anyway, who cares as long as it doesn't concern us—
we say.
But it concerns the forty-eight dead passengers,
Their near and dear ones:
All destined to be victims of the failure of a mere
automation
Or a callous hand that had a few pegs of whisky
Before taking to the wheels.
Today, the machine has claimed its due share again
And man who had built it for his own comfort and use
Will continue to amortize the cost of living with death,
Peace with war, and progress with self-destruction.
A few will mourn or write a dirge like this poet,
But the rest will forget the whole damn thing in a few
days—
Apropos our collective amnesia born of ennui
And the meaningless rituals of modern life.
While someone amongst us will laugh all the way to the
bank
With the insurance money of the damaged vehicle!

Nota Bene: A very tragic accident occurred when a private city bus fell into a gorge between Itanagar and Naharlagun, the twin towns of the state capital of Arunachal Pradesh on 22 May 2004, killing forty-eight people on board. It happened during the peak traffic hour, and many saw the whole tragedy unfolding in front of their eyes.

Maybe This Man

Maybe this man
Who is so partial
In his dealings is misunderstood by me.
After all,
Even I suffer the habit
Of preferring one thing over another—
Preferring to stay at home with my children on
holidays,
Enjoying a good read to a blockbuster movie,
Supporting Real Madrid FC,
Enthusiastic about Van Gogh,
Always biased in favour of the underdogs,
Rooting for the dark horses to come up trumps
On many occasions,
And also having a very sweet tooth.

MOLLYCODDLED
LITTLE CHILDREN

Mollycoddled little children
Of the neighbourhood
Throw tantrums,
Bicker and fight with one another,
Only to make up
Over a few apologetic words
And a bashful grin.
They line up all along the road
Winding up the Apatani plateau
Like the pine trees,
Slender and evergreen
And wave at our passing cavalcade.
Our hearts like mollycoddled children,
Throwing tantrums,
Bickering and fighting,
But also giving us VIP treatment,
Waving at our passing cavalcade.

AT NIGHT I SEE THE BEAST STALKING THE HILLS

At night I see the beast stalking the hills
Whose hands like the wind comb the forest;
And whose velutinous body is trapped with desire,
Twisting and turning like the rivulet
Eager to race down the valley.
At a distance, cymbals clamping sharply
From the prayer halls
Reach a crescendo;
Amidst the rumble of chants
From the monks in their saffron clothes.
A lithe doe scampers for cover
Into the shadow of the trees,
Insatiate—
As the hot summer night crackles
Under the weight of its own lust.

THE VANDALS BROKE IN AND RANSACKED MY PLACE

The vandals broke in and ransacked my place
And left emptiness gnawing at me,
With cockroaches scurrying through the floor,
Climbing up bamboo poles,
Getting into every nook and cranny
Of the split-bamboo house
In gossamer feet,
And the mice getting violent,
Emptying every little container for food.
I have nothing
Left for you—
I have lost all my treasures to someone
Who robbed me so thoroughly.

LIKE THE SAP OF A TUBER PLANT

Like the sap of a tuber plant
You have permeated me—
I am so full
Of you
And by you.
I long for you
With an aching heart.
Everything I pick up
Is marked with your initials,
The perfume you like
And some old habits of mine that you dislike—
For instance,
When I belch
And pet the tummy after a meal.

THE FEATHER OF
THE HORNBILL

The feather of the hornbill—
The downy hides of a dead tiger—
Its fangs.
The clipped wings of an eagle—
Its claws—its eyes—
Its beaks.
You can have everything
The poor animals and birds have to offer—
To make a pouch, a headgear,
A hunting trophy for display in your living room.
But can you map the thrill of its flight
Or own what belongs to it truly,
Which is the spirit:
The spirit you cannot kill,
And it often resides in a weak body.

DAWKI

You will be remembered
As the place where the twain did meet for a moment
That day—
A spark of fire meeting a giant iceberg—
You can say it was a good melting experience
And a beautiful warming experience.
Your green waters calmly spilling over to the *Bangla*
On whose either banks people bath and wash clothes
As children frolic in the hot sand,
While fishermen glide like statues in their boats
Under the fierce vigil of the moustached sentry
Pointing away his gun at the distance.
It was just a three-hour picnic
But enough to last a lifetime.
It was enough talking to her
In the silent speech of your tongue,
Where the boundaries blurred between two hostile
nations,
Even as two hearts blended securely
With the blue and viridian of the landscape.

Nota Bene: Dawki is a border town between the Indian
state of Meghalaya and Bangladesh.

MYTH MAKING

I see something else besides the rotating fan,
Chairs, teacups on the table,
And the men glued to the TV set in the room.
Something more vivid than the objects around me.
In the dark like a statue coming to life
To the full glare of the inner eye,
A hideous, scaly, green monster
With thorns growing on its body like cactus darts up
Riveting me to the wall.
And even as my eyes pop out
And the hairs stand on their follicles,
A serpentine smell fills the air
While every detail around me
Is fudged like the broken lens of an old camera—
The focus waxing and waning
And then finally substantiating
Into a vista of vast landscape in white, teal blue, and
emerald,
Perched on whose soft bosom is a sleepy little hamlet,
Where an old patriarch,
Sitting in the courtyard is spinning tales of the dragon,
Solid as the mountain,
Pregnant with volcano,
Smoking fire from the pits of its cavernous belly

And a group of boys suspending belief for a moment,
Willingly lap up every concoction of the old master at
play
In the timeless art of myth making.
The old stuff haunts us even today
Like the grudging spirit of the dead;
Have our reasoning mind in thralls—
So that it believes in the distortion of facts,
With the dogged habit of customs and traditions;
Sometimes with the sanctity of a primitive religion,
Befooling man to worshipping stones,
Even as it unstones to become a god.

DEAD FISH

Let the bird fly.
You cannot say that from now onwards
It must walk on its soft feet
As if the blue sky is bounded.
I tell you
There is enough for all of us—
The birds that fly will tell you.
You may have a big ego
But the creator has made a bigger universe
In which you are a small part.
But each one of us is unique.
It's a fact that must be accepted with humility and
grace.
Put a fish out of water,
It will beat about the ground
Till out of breath it dies on land.
It is the creature of the sea
And in the deep finds the lap of a mother
And the heart of a lover.
The reclusive painter is happy
To mine beauty in colours and forms.
At work he is inspired
Or else he is lifeless like the dead fish.
And the poet will not be silenced.

The strongman cannot bend him
Or break him.
On the other hand
With a renewed vigour
He will speak out for the poor and destitute
Of all places and times—
For he has known nothing,
Save to sing the song of victory
In the land of the displaced and the oppressed.

EUTHANASIA

I will gag the mouth and suffocate it—
Lest the cry bring in the whole neighbourhood to my
place,
With eyes dissecting my character in fine details,
Like a group of boys gleefully
Splitting the innards of a wet green frog in a school lab.
With my bare hands
I will wring its neck, twist and turn it,
And the final release will come
When it flaps its wings and kicks its feet
And the heart will cease to beat, beat and cease to a full
stop—
I wish I could give my feelings a painless death.

A VILLAGE BELLE'S
LOVE LETTER

I

You sent me billet-doux
I could not read,
But I understood the language of the heart,
The shape of your words and the colour of your
emotions:
Those are not bounded by the rules of any grammar,
Nor beholden to any of your ABCs.
I have allowed none to read them for me.
I have kept my emotions to myself alone,
Pressing them to my bosom,
Nurturing them in a twilight zone
Of propriety and gullibility.
I implore you:
Come to me any time,
Make my heart your permanent dwelling
Where the star people visit me with their music in the
night
And during the day steal away with everything I own—
All my joys, my wealth, my very disposition!
Your wide gaze that follow me to the ends of the earth,
Your scented breath that bathe me in its aroma,

Your fair skin glowing like the moon,
Your kindness, your name which I chant like a prayer;
Everything about you
Has filled me to such an extent
That I am full of you.
I wish I could hold up the sky for you to see
How I look at you,
As someone with a swell heart.

II

You sent me billet-doux.
I have hid it in the folds of my garments,
Afraid of the world
That never takes kindly to lovers:
I was afraid of our parents' objection,
I was afraid of neighbours gossiping about us,
I was afraid of friends teasing me no end,
I was afraid of the headman's daughter
Who has her eyes on you,
I was also afraid of you
Who was brought up in the wayward ways of the
city boy—
For I heard that love for the city folks is a pastime
Like a game of cards,
For laying a wager on people's sentiments
And preying on their vulnerability.
Yet something happened to me
When I got a letter
Bearing your initials,
That I forgot sleep

And sleeping could not wake from that beautiful dream
Seeing us
Walk off
To the sun
Hand in hand
Together,
Happily ever after,
As in the Bollywood movies.

BETWEEN YOU AND ME

(The Gypsy, Spelunker, and the
Anthropomorphic Entity)

1. The Gypsy

In the sands of time
Was an oasis:
Out there, somewhere,
In a world of innate possibilities
On a given day.
You can call it fate
Or a stroke of good fortune.
It may even be that I willed it to happen—
Desired that my caravan stop by,
To provision and recuperate
Before marching onward the voyage to eternity.
You were there too,
My gypsy girl,
As part of the entourage of an ancient tribe
Sojourning through these tracts
Of subterfuge and naught,
Strewn with the relics of a lost age.
You were there,
Standing apart from everything and everyone else

In a sea of people
Coming and going.
The moment caught in an epiphany
When eyes met eyes
And your soul calling out to me:
'Let us build for ourselves a nest.
Our little ones need to grow strong wings
Before they can fly
And build one for themselves too.'
I heard your voice
Above the din this mundane world makes
To feel alive and kicking;
Above the sounds of myself
Functioning like a clockwork—
For a moment, I ceased ticking
To hear you,
Alone—
Apart from everything else around—
Just you and me,
Two lonely people in the universe
On the threshold of an exciting journey
Into each other's hearts.
Your voice calling out to me
As I lay drowning
In a sea of mediocrity and spite
Losing grip of reality
Losing grip of I, me, and myself
Your voice bringing me back to the light—
This gypsy has been taught
To value this life with you

In the oasis
Where I have built a world around you, my love.
You said, 'Let's build our nest on top of the tallest tree
In this oasis,
Where we have sought each other out,
We of all the people on earth,
To fall in love in a place where life is so ephemeral.

'Let's build our nest on top of the most sturdy tree,
Whose roots manacle the shifty sand dunes
And tame it to servitude and fixity.
Let's stop for a moment here
To see time's arrow fall from their trajectory
And land in our lap,
To see the seasons caught in a hora of endless cycle
And die in our arms,
Like some distant stars dying on each other
On an unknown galaxy far, far away.'

2. Spelunker

This spelunker
Having charted the terrains of underground caves
Knows their mud, their beautiful rock formations;
Their high pitches and tight crawl ways;
Their awesome but fragile ecosystems;
Knows the dogged determination with which the river
Bored through their rocks over the years
To meet the sea.
The journey to the bottom of your heart

Is a similar story;
Of pursuit and pain;
Of adventure and discovery;
Of fall and rise.
Ask of sea for the seeds of sorrows
Sown in separation
And also the bitter fruits
Reaped in waiting—
Bitter fruits that heal souls.
Ask it to lay bare its feelings,
So that men who believe in destiny,
In the cycle of separation and union,
Are salvaged from the wreckages of misfortune in time.

3. Anthropomorphic Entity

My heart is like a stuffed toy.
A cute-looking teddy bear
With a blue- silk ribbon tied around its neck.
Its marble eyes it had only for you,
Following the direction of your gaze,
Everywhere you went.
It could not come to you (though it would have
liked to);
You came to it whenever you wanted
But made it wait for you patiently for days at home.
Its ears it had only to hear you out;
Even though it had a mouth, it could not speak to you
Because a toy is not supposed to speak
Even when spoken to.

Its winsome visage ever ready to be showered with
kisses.
Its soft, warm brown body at a moment's notice
Ready to receive you in a bear hug.
It existed to pander to all your whimsies and desires.
You played with it; you befriended it.
You endowed it with feelings . . . yes, special feelings
for yourself.
This anthropomorphic entity
Made the mistake of taking you too far seriously.
It did not calculate you would grow up someday,
That the baubles and trinkets of childhood days
Would lose their relevance for you
In changed circumstances.

An Irreligious Man Conscious of His Sins

I suffer the silence of prayer—
My soul held in its vice-like grip,
My guilt-filled mind wincing in pain,
And with every pronouncement,
Like denouncements,
Of the clergy in habit,
From the height of the pulpit,
I am condemned
To the bottomless pit of Hades!

Cul-de-Sac

The dead left nothing to chance;
No firm grip on the rock face to climb—
Smooth surface and treacherous height;
No beaten track leading to any of their secret
assignations—
Nothing was left—no records of anything at all.
The rhapsodists only lead us up to a point and leave us
there
—Alone.
Their songs and their prayers merely clues to other clues
(With also clues in them),
But getting us nowhere really.
Is it nostalgia? Perhaps, not the right word
For a tribe trying to chart the lost city
Never built by their ancestors,
Where the seeds of a new sun were sown,
The pheromones of whose fissile nature
Could put to shame the fecundity of any virgin.
I am resolved to find the keys and coordinates
In the heart of the shaman's chants,
In the entrails of the sacrificial beast,
In the yolk of the egg,
In the stories of our dead ancestors,
Their lamentations and their love songs.

But every time I near it,
I am banished from the familiar mien of the truth
That shaped the tribe's outlook,
Their world view,
The circumstance of their close encounter with the gods,
Who dwell on the high mountains of the land,
The deep forest, and the swift rivers.
Am I in exile?
Exile is a fourteen-years-long word,
Where every second mutates to the eternity of a god's
cycle.
In exile, I have died a thousand times
In every tick of its clock's hand
Banished from people known and loved by me.
These mountains, abode of our gods,
Haunt of my exile, stand tall in their pristine glory
And fill me with awe and grandeur.
But in the dark
When the peaks tower like giant druid stones
Gathered for a secret session of seance
In a bid to unlock the night's mystery,
Prying eyes and scurrying feet
With ravenous hunger that make brutes eat their litter,
Induce unease in the umbra of its gaping maw.
Such moments of disquiet suffers poetry to hack its ten
heads—
Just for the heck of it.
So that the acephalous being only thinks of survival:
This primeval instinct overpowers everything else,
As life in the wild can be cruel and unfeeling.

THE OLD FART

Listen to the low moan of the moon
Sending a shudder down the spine of the mountains,
Where it wishes to dip its diaphanous wings
Into the frigid lakes dotting the commanding heights,
Whose veneer of false modesty
Now puts off the old fellow.
You see,
It wants to walk with me
On the small path
Leading up to my village
On the berm—
The path where my forefathers have trodden
Gratefully
On the face of this earth—
Now unused by this generation
That has built a wide modern road
Of asphalt and concrete for itself.
It wants to kiss the snow-capped mountains
Where the spirits dwell (good and bad,
Meddlesome and apathetic)
Shaping the lives of our people
And who in turn appease the numen
With their offerings

Scattered everywhere
By the singing wind—
The seeds sprout
And raise their heads in the fog
And disappear without trace
Into the pall
Along with it the burden
Of our ancient faith.
It wants to run and play
With the swift rivers and streams
Flowing through the wooded massif,
Our impregnable fort of isolation and perpetuation.
It wants to join in the fellowship
Of our songs and dances,
Our ceremonies of birth and mourning,
In our most intimate moments
Of love and longings,
Amorous and passionate.
The mountains
Are now littered
By this heathen generation
With the detritus of their fun and frolic
And the drying rivers are choked
By the flotsam and jetsam
From the great cities and their conurbations,
Which really, really puts off the old fart.
These days no one believes
That the almighty sun and moon,
Worshipped by our people,

Are demiurgical godheads.
In the age of space rocket and nuclear science,
In the information age,
No one talks such nonsense now.

LET'S HOPE ANYWAY

Someday,
You will come back to me
As does the Bos frontalis,
Piebald and white-faced,
Returns to its salt licks
Tucked away in the core of cool earth
And green copses:
Maybe
Then,
I will lead you
Back,
Salt-licking,
To my house—
And it will be your second coming.

Nota Bene: The Bos frontalis (Mithun) is a semi-domesticated cattle wealth of the Nyishi tribe. It is allowed to roam freely around a habitat with a salt lick from where the owner leads it to the village luring it with a handful of salts.

To Bo Senior

When the waters
Reached out to grab you,
You ran to the hills
And climbed up the trees
To save yourself
And your race
From extinction.
Your tribal instinct told you
That you must run to the hills
As up there
We have always felt safe and secure
From our enemies
For countless centuries,
Where the soaring eagle
Tries to tear apart
The wind
But drops back
To the earth,
Where the clouds
Hang so close in the blue sky—
So close that you can have
A clutch of the shaggy fleeces
In your hand,
Where the sun rises like the giant ball of fire

And hurtles down
On the other side of the mountain
To rise again
In the land of the dead
Where our ancestors
Wait for us.
You ran and ran,
Till you were out of breath
And your legs gave away.
You were resolved
That your people
Live through you
And from you
To tell the world
About your unique civilization.
You ran the race of your life
For the children
Whom you should have brought
To this world,
To celebrate life
And all the meaningless rituals
Of the living.
In the end
You lost out.
But I don't think
It was all in vain
And without some purpose.
Surely, the creator of the universe
Had some purpose

In his scheme of things,
When he unleashed
You and your fellow tribesmen
To this world.

Nota Bene: Boa Sr. (*circa* 1925 – 26 January 2010[1])
was an Indian Great Andamanese elder. She was the last
surviving person who remembered any Bo, a language
of the Great Andamanese language family.
She survived the Asian tsunami of 2014 by climbing up
a tree but many of her people were not as fortunate as
her.

About the Author

Yumlam Tana, belongs to the Nyishi tribe who share a common ancestry in the mythological figure of Abotani with the Adi, Apatani, Galo, Tagin tribes of Arunachal Pradesh and the Mishings of Assam.

He is at present working as Deputy Director of School Education in the Department of Education, Government of Arunachal Pradesh and lives in Jully, Itanagar, Arunachal Pradesh.

He is also the author of 'The Man and the Tiger' (published by The Writers Forum, Ranchi) and two comic books on Nyishi mythological tales, 'The Wooing of Jiwt' and 'The Struggle for Existence'.

He was also previously nominated as member of India's national and regional art and cultural bodies like Lalit Kala Akademi, New Delhi and North East Zone Cultural Center, Dimapur.

Printed in the United States
By Bookmasters